$2

D0099897

Jesus A to Z

Michael O'Neill McGrath, OSFS

Michael McGrath

Christmas 2007

WLP

WORLD LIBRARY PUBLICATIONS

Franklin Park, Illinois

Jesus A to Z © 2007, World Library Publications, the music and liturgy
division of J.S. Paluch Company, Inc., 3708 River Road, Suite 400,
Franklin Park, Illinois 60131-2158
800 566-6150 • www.wlpmusic.com

All rights reserved under United States copyright law. No part of this book
may be reproduced or transmitted in any form or by any means, mechanical,
photographic, or electronic, including photocopying, or any information
storage or retrieval system, without the written permission of the
appropriate copyright owner.

Google™ is a trademark of Google, Inc.

Art and commentary by Michael O'Neill McGrath © 2007, World Library Publications.

The paintings were done in acrylics on watercolor paper.

This book was edited by Christine Krzystofczyk with assistance from
Alan J. Hommerding and Marcia T. Lucey. Editorial consultation by Christine Ondrla.
Design and layout by Christine Enault. Production manager was Deb Johnston. The book
was set in Berkeley Oldstyle, Berliner Grotesk, and ITC Garamond. Printed in South Korea.
Graphics TwoFortyFour Inc.

WLP 007199   ISBN 978-1-58459-332-4

Michael O'Neill McGrath, OSFS

_____

Acts 1:1–11

A   All the apostles at the Ascension

Galatians 3:26–28

Bountiful blessings for babies at baptism

B

Psalm 96:11–13

C Children's choir conducted in Christmas carols

Matthew 28:18–20

Diverse disciples directed by divine dove to distant destinations **D**

Revelation 1:1–3

E   Evangelists enjoy an exciting Easter egg expedition

John 21:1–14

Jesus flipped fried fish for his friends

F

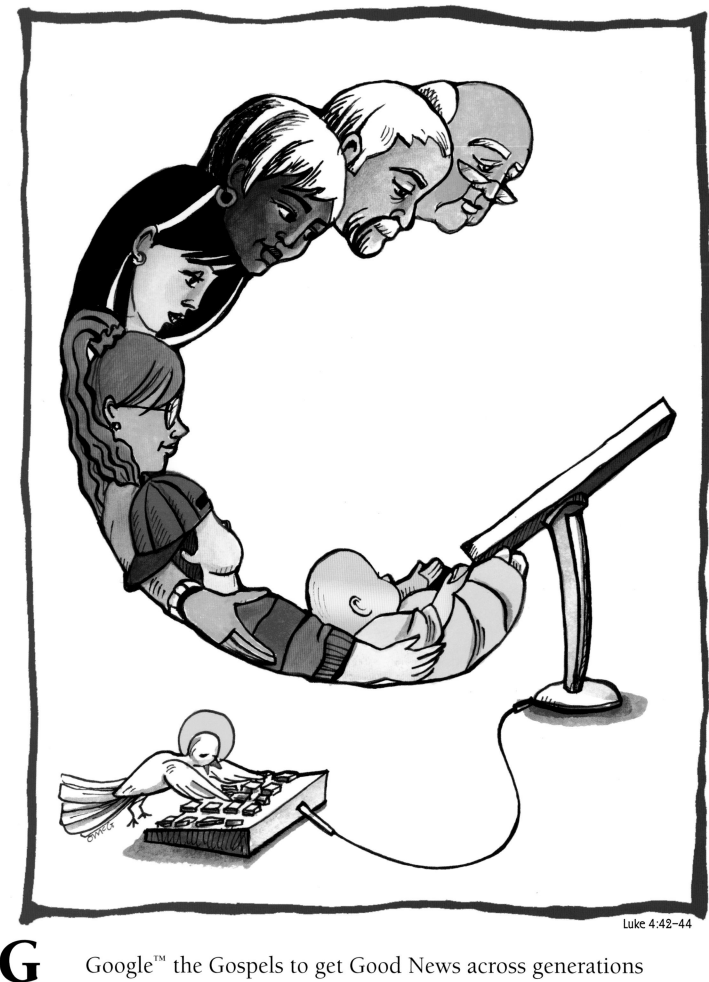

Luke 4:42–44

G Google™ the Gospels to get Good News across generations

Revelation 4:8

Heavenly hosts with harps and horns holler Hosanna and Hallelujah

Psalm 141:2

I

Icon images inhaling incense

Luke 2:41–52

Jesus journeys to Jerusalem with Joseph

J

Matthew 16:15–19

K   The kindly King with keys to the kingdom

John 11:1–44

The Lord leads Lazarus to leap to life

L

Luke 10:38–42

M Mary and Martha made many meals for the Messiah

Luke 2:1–14

Noisy noels were noted at the Nativity

N

James 5:14–15

O Oil for sacraments originates in ordinary olives

John 12:12–16

A parade of people with palms praises Jesus

P

Psalm 45:10, 11, 12, 16

Q The Queen requests quiet for her Son's quick nap

Mark 16:1–7

The Redeemer arose at the Resurrection

R

John 10:11–18

S   The Shepherd seeks straying sheep

Matthew 17:1–9

A trembling trio transfixed by the Transfiguration

T

Matthew 5:3–10

U

Jesus loves the unclean, unhealthy, and unloved

Romans 12:9–21

Vices vanish when virtue is victorious

V

 Waiters watched water turn to wine at a wedding

Luke 2:13–14

In excelsis Deo is exclaimed in extremely far galaxies

X

Y

Youngsters yell yippee with Yeshua

Mark 10:13–16

Luke 19:1–10

Zacchaeus zoomed up a tree to gaze at Jesus from its zenith

Z

ABC GLOSSARY

To Parents, Grandparents, Godparents, and Other Teachers

Just in case you feel a little rusty on some of the terms illustrated in this alphabet, this glossary has been included for you. In addition to some basic definitions, there are little conversation starters to help you and your child see the connection between ordinary, everyday life and these sacred stories and symbols of our faith.

Ascension: The time when Jesus went home to heaven, body and all, while the apostles watched. The apostles were Jesus' twelve closest friends. They traveled with him and witnessed his life and death, and Jesus trusted them to tell others about him.

Did you ever have to say good-bye to someone? Do you have a happy memory that keeps that person with you?

Baptism: The sacrament that welcomes babies, and older people as well, into the Church as children of God. Butterflies are symbols of new life because they come out of cocoons after they have been changed.

Ask an adult to tell the story of your baptism. Who are your godparents?

Christmas carols: Songs that remind us that Jesus was born on Christmas day. Christmas carols always tell us two things: Jesus was born as a human baby, and that little human baby was also God.

What is your favorite Christmas carol? Why?

Disciples: Friends and followers of Jesus from all over the world who use their talents and gifts to spread the gospel.

What gifts do you share as a disciple? How many diverse people can you identify?

Evangelists: The four writers who were the first to record the stories (Gospels) of Jesus. Their names are Matthew, Mark, Luke, and John.

Read the beginning of each Gospel in your Bible. How are they different? How are they alike?

Fish: A symbol for Jesus from the earliest times. Fish was a popular food in Jesus' day, so he would have eaten it often with his friends. Once after his resurrection, Jesus cooked fish as a special breakfast for the apostles.

What would you make for breakfast for Jesus? Why?

Gospel: The Gospels are the written stories of Jesus' life and mission on earth. "Gospel" means "good news." We can learn the Gospel stories from the Bible, from books, in church, or from our family and teachers. We can even find them on the Internet!

How many generations are in your family? Name as many relatives as you can. Remember to include the ones you don't like so much, because Jesus loves them as much as he loves you.

Heavenly host: Another name for all the angels who sing "Holy, holy, holy" and who sing all the time around God's throne in heaven. The heavenly host sang in the sky over Bethlehem when Jesus was born.

What makes you so happy that you want to sing and shout hallelujah or hooray?

Incense: A perfumed substance that we burn to make a beautiful smell in church. Our prayers rise up to God like the smoke from the incense.

What are your five senses? How can each of them be used to pray?

Journey: When he was a boy, Jesus went to the holy city of Jerusalem for special feast days, traveling with St. Joseph because boys traveled with their fathers and girls traveled with their mothers. Once, when he was twelve years old, he got lost, but his parents found him in the Temple.

Have you ever gone on a special journey or pilgrimage with your parents? Where?

Keys to the Kingdom: Jesus once gave St. Peter the keys to the Kingdom, but here he gives them to everyone to show us the way to heaven. Sometimes Jesus is shown as a little boy king and is called the Holy Child.

Name some things that need keys to open them. What do you think "unlocks" the kingdom of God on earth?

Lazarus: Jesus was so sad when his friend Lazarus died that he cried at Lazarus' tomb. Then he performed a great miracle and raised his friend from the dead.

Have you ever known someone who died? How did you feel? Can you share a story about the person who died?

Mary and Martha: Lazarus had two sisters, Mary and Martha, who were also close friends of Jesus. They used to invite Jesus over for dinner and visits to their home in Bethany.

When does your family have special-occasion dinners? Do guests come to your house or do you go visit other families?

Noels: Another word for Christmas songs. Even all the animals were so excited about Jesus' birth that they made whatever noises they could to show their joy.

Make as many animal sounds as you can. Get lots of other people to join in, until it sounds like Noah's ark!

Together, try to find and list as many items as you can in each picture that begin with the letter depicted (don't forget to include shapes and colors, too). In the lower corner of each drawing is a scriptural citation that may be of help to you in locating a biblical source or inspiration for the image. And be sure to look for the Holy Spirit, who appears as a little dove somewhere in each scene.

Olive oil: In Jesus' day it was common to rub oil on people's foreheads to show that they were special in the eyes of God. Today we anoint people with oil in some sacraments: baptism, confirmation, holy orders, and anointing of the sick.

Do you have some olive oil in your house? Have an adult put some on your fingers. Smell it and dab a little on your own forehead or someone else's.

Palm Sunday: Jesus rode into Jerusalem on a donkey the week before he died. The people were so excited to see him that they waved palm branches at him as he passed by, like we do today with confetti.

Whom would you cheer for today? Is it because they are like Jesus?

Queen: Mary is sometimes called the Queen of Heaven because her Son, Jesus, is the King of Heaven. When a painting shows her holding Jesus as a baby or little boy, the picture is called a "Madonna and Child."

Do you know how to pray the rosary to honor Mary?

Resurrection: Jesus died on Good Friday, but he came back to life and rose from the dead on Easter Sunday morning. Three of his friends—Mary Magdalene, Mary the mother of James, and Salome—went to visit his tomb, where an angel told them the good news.

What are your favorite Easter traditions and customs?

Shepherd: Jesus often called us his flock and himself the Good Shepherd. This title reminds us that we are all like sheep who sometimes get lost, but Jesus will always go looking for us.

Have you ever been lost or afraid? Who came to find you or comfort you? That person was like a "shepherd" for a "lost sheep."

Transfiguration: One time Jesus took three friends—Peter, James, and John—to the top of a mountain and appeared before them in a dazzling light with Moses and the prophet Elijah. The three apostles were so amazed that they trembled and fell down. Peter wanted to put up tents on the spot so everyone could stay up on the mountain.

Have you ever gotten dressed up and somebody said, "I didn't recognize you!" How did you feel? Why don't we stay dressed up all the time? Why do you think Jesus came down from the mountain to go back to work among the people?

Un- . . . : Jesus has great love for anyone who is unpopular and needs a friend or is unwell and needs good health. He has special love for people who are poor or who have special needs.

Do you know any people who have special needs? Is there any way you can help them?

Virtue and vice: Sometimes it is hard to do what we know is good and right (virtue) when the wrong choice (vice) appears to be more fun or appealing.

When can you do something virtuous when a vice is so tempting?

Water and wine: Once Jesus and his mother went to a wedding in a town called Cana. When the bride and groom ran out of wine to serve their guests, he performed his first miracle by turning water into wine.

Have you ever been to a wedding or another big party? Why wouldn't you want to run out of food or drink for the guests?

In excelsis Deo: Angels sang Gloria in excelsis Deo! on Christmas night. It means "Glory to God in the highest"—even out in space!

What wonderful (or even small) things make you want to sing praise to God?

Youngsters: Yeshua is Jesus' name in Aramaic, his native language. Jesus loved little children and always let them come close so he could bless them and tell them stories. He once said that everyone, even grownups, had to be like little children to enter heaven.

What do you think Jesus meant by "be like a child"? Do you know anyone like that?

Zacchaeus: He was too short to see Jesus in the crowd, so he climbed a tree to get a better look. Jesus told him to come down, that he would stay and eat dinner at his house.

Would you climb a tree or the monkey bars to see Jesus if he came to your neighborhood? Why or why not?

Brother **Mickey McGrath** is an Oblate of St. Francis de Sales and an award-winning artist and author. Ever since he can remember he has loved to draw and paint. He thinks that art is a fun and unique way to pray and spread the gospel. His paintings and stories of Jesus, Mary, and the saints have appeared in many books and articles, most notably including *Blessed Art Thou* and *At the Name of Jesus.* When he's not painting, Brother Mickey brings the gospel of art to teachers and students of all ages in retreats and presentations throughout the United States.

MARK WINTERBOTTOM, OSFS

A note from the artist...
Bro. Mickey McGrath

From its earliest days, Christianity has been a religious tradition that uses words and images to teach the faith as well as to inspire the faithful to prayer and meditation. This book flows right out of that tradition, drawing on and honoring the old but presenting it in a new way. The clothes and computers may change, but the basic message of God incarnate in our world remains timeless. I hope this book helps you and your child discover a new face of God, one who smiles at us and encourages delight in the ordinary.